PU

ROUGH

Here is a lively antholo... and girls, full of the worst behaviour and the wickedest deeds imaginable. There are stories about spoiled Veruca Salt who tries to steal a squirrel from the Nut Room, Little Alpesh who causes all sorts of trouble with his conker, and Harriet who takes a crocodile on the bus in her schoolbag. Mixed with limericks, light-hearted verses and hilarious illustrations, this is an irresistible collection with a cast of characters no one will forget.

Anne Wood founded the independent magazine for parents, *Books For Your Children*. She received the Eleanor Farjeon Award for services to children's literature in 1969 and has also won prizes for television production. She now runs her own company, Ragdoll Productions, specializing in programmes for children and books relating to them. She is Founder President of the Federation of Children's Book Groups, the organization for parents concerned to find out more about children's books.

George English is a freelance broadcaster who has produced a weekly children's book feature for Radio Newcastle for over ten years. He has contributed to many periodicals on the subject of children's books.

Rough and Tumble

Edited by Anne Wood and George English

Illustrated by Judy Brown

PUFFIN BOOKS

PUFFIN BOOKS

Published by the Penguin Group
Penguin Books Ltd, 27 Wrights Lane, London W8 5TZ, England
Penguin Books USA Inc., 375 Hudson Street, New York, New York 10014, USA
Penguin Books Australia Ltd, Ringwood, Victoria, Australia
Penguin Books Canada Ltd, 10 Alcorn Avenue, Toronto, Ontario, Canada M4V 3B2
Penguin Books (NZ) Ltd, 182–190 Wairau Road, Auckland 10, New Zealand

Penguin Books Ltd, Registered Offices: Harmondsworth, Middlesex, England

First published by Viking 1990
Published in Puffin Books 1991
3 5 7 9 10 8 6 4

This selection copyright © Anne Wood and George English, 1990
Illustrations copyright © Judy Brown, 1990
All rights reserved

Printed in England by Clays Ltd, St Ives plc

Except in the United States of America, this book is sold subject
to the condition that it shall not, by way of trade or otherwise, be lent,
re-sold, hired out, or otherwise circulated without the publisher's
prior consent in any form of binding or cover other than that in
which it is published and without a similar condition including this
condition being imposed on the subsequent purchaser

Contents

The Croco-bus . Martin Waddell
8

The Conker as Hard as a Diamond . Chris Powling
14

Veruca in the Nut Room . Roald Dahl
22

Castles in the Sand . David Henry Wilson
30

Temper, Temper . . . Jules Older
35

In the Larder . Marion St John Webb
42

The Secret . Gene Kemp
47

When Emil Got His Head
Stuck in the Soup Tureen . Astrid Lindgren
52

Marmalade and Rufus at the Ritz . Andrew Davies
59

Friends and Brothers . Dick King-Smith
73

Acknowledgements
79

Bad
(After Michael Jackson)

Bad on Monday,
Bad on Tuesday,
Bad all day today,
Bad on Thursday,
Bad on Friday,
Can't go out to play.

Can't go to the pictures,
Or even out to swim,
Can't go out with Harriet,
Or even out with Jim.

Bad on Monday,
Bad on Tuesday,
Bad all day today,
Bad on Thursday,
Bad on Friday,
I can't go out to play.

Come off it mum it's very sad,
I can't go riding on my bike,
And all because of being bad,
I can't do anything I like.

Bad on Monday,
Bad on Tuesday,
Bad all day today,
Bad on Thursday,
Bad on Friday,
It's pretty bad I say.

George English

The Croco-bus

Martin Waddell

'We can't take a crocodile on the bus, Harriet,' said Anthea anxiously. 'The busman won't like it.'

'Nonsense,' said Harriet, hitching up her wriggling schoolbag.

Harriet's schoolbag didn't usually wriggle. It was wriggling this time because there was a crocodile inside it, eating.

The crocodile was a smallish, friendly crocodile. He had been pottering around his cage looking for another smaller crocodile to eat when Harriet whistled at him.

Harriet's whistle wasn't an ordinary whistle. It was the special Snail Whistle that she used for Training her World Champion. It worked on snails, and it worked on the crocodile.

The crocodile moved toward her as if he was hypnotized. The next thing he knew, he was inside Harriet's schoolbag, nestling up to her lunchbox and eating her jotter. By the time Harriet reached the bus-stop, he had eaten her Maths book and her pencil case and was making a start on her beret, which was indigestible even for a crocodile with a strong stomach.

'Now we've got it, what do we do with it?' Anthea asked, standing on the side of Harriet which was furthest from the wriggling schoolbag.

'Take it home,' said Harriet.

Which is why they were waiting at the bus-stop opposite the Zoo for the bus back into town.

'What about the others?' said Anthea. 'They'll think we're lost.'

Harriet took no notice. She went back to whistling at her crocodile.

Harriet was a good whistler. Her whistle soothed the little

crocodile. He stopped wriggling and swallowed the last shreds of the beret. So long as Harriet kept whistling, he was a happy crocodile.

The bus came.

Harriet and Anthea got on, and went to sit on the top deck.

'There's room beside me,' Harriet said, when Anthea made a point of sitting three seats away, just in case.

'I prefer to sit by myself, thank you very much, Harriet,' said Anthea, who was worried about what might happen next.

'Now then, now then! Stop that whistling!' shouted the conductor, up the stairs.

Harriet stopped.

Her schoolbag started wriggling.

Harriet started again.

The conductor came pounding up the stairs.

'Stop that whistling! You're annoying the other passengers,' the conductor said, advancing down the aisle.

'No I'm not,' said Harriet.

'Oh yes you are,' said the conductor, coming to a stop beside her. 'This is my bus, and I won't have you whistling on it.'

Harriet shrugged, and stopped whistling.

The schoolbag gave a gentle wriggle.

The conductor blinked.

'Two tens please,' said Anthea quickly, thrusting the bus money at him in the hope that she could divert his attention.

'What's that?' said the conductor, pointing at Harriet's wriggling schoolbag. Harriet had taken the schoolbag off when she got on the bus, because the crocodile was rather heavy. Now, with each wriggle, it was inching its way across the seat.

'My schoolbag,' said Harriet.

The schoolbag gave a grunt.

Harriet grabbed at the strap, and pursed her mouth to whistle, in the hope that the crocodile would stop wriggling.

'You've got livestock in that!' said the conductor. 'No livestock allowed on my bus without special permission. I won't have it!'

'You wouldn't *want* it, if you had,' said Anthea bitterly, but no one heard her.

'Evading fares!' said the conductor, getting quite worked up. 'Carrying undeclared livestock on a Corporation Vehicle without paying the appropriate fare is an Offence under Rule 4 subsection 3 of the Corporation Bye-laws, Public Omnibus Regulations 1948.' He grabbed the wriggling schoolbag, and held it aloft.

'You're caught, you are!' he cried, triumphantly. 'I call on all my passengers to be witnesses!'

The two men and three boys who were on the top deck took one look at the schoolbag and one look at Harriet and got off.

'I saw *teeth*,' one of them muttered, as he ran down the stairs.

'Now then, now then, Miss. I'll have your particulars, if you don't mind,' said the conductor. And he put down the schoolbag on the floor, and got out his notebook.

Anthea turned pale.

There was a loud chewing noise coming from the schoolbag. A green snout, edged with sharp teeth, emerged through the side of the bag. It was a leather bag, best quality, purchased by Harriet's Auntie Clemence in Ostend on a Works Trip, and the crocodile found it very tasty indeed.

'Name?' said the conductor.

'Harriet,' said Harriet.

'H ... A ... *Harriet*?' said the conductor, suddenly turning pale.

He put down his pencil and took a closer look at Harriet.

He had seen her somewhere before.

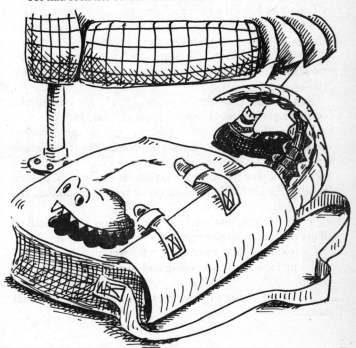

'Not . . . not THE Harriet?' he gurgled, panic stricken.

But he knew it was, without Harriet saying anything.

Harriet's picture, front and side face, was displayed on a Warning Notice with Big Red Letters stuck up on the Corporation Bus Staff Regulations and Timetables Notice Board.

The bus conductor retreated.

It was the wisest thing to do, confronted by Harriet, but unfortunately he retreated over Harriet's schoolbag, which he had put down on the floor.

Part of Harriet's schoolbag. *Most* of Harriet's schoolbag was already inside the crocodile. He had eaten his way out to look for his Big Green Mum who had stopped whistling. He felt lonely, and when he felt lonely, he got hungry.

The crocodile was looking round for something to have a cosy chew at when the bus conductor's trouser leg, complete with sock, shoe, foot and ankle, presented itself, going backwards.

SNAP!

'Aaaaaaaah!' screamed the bus conductor, and he fainted clean away.

'Oh dear,' said Harriet.

'I think perhaps we'd better get off the bus, Harriet,' said Anthea.

Harriet scooped up her crocodile and stuffed it down inside her cardigan.

Then she got off the bus, whistling softly to keep her crocodile happy.

Noise

Billy is blowing his trumpet;
Bertie is banging a tin;
Betty is crying for mummy
And Bob has pricked Ben with a pin.
Baby is crying out loudly;
He's out on the lawn in his pram.
I am the only one silent
And I've eaten all of the jam.

Anon.

The Conker as Hard as a Diamond

Chris Powling

Apart from its fancy box it didn't look at all special. What was there to make Little Alpesh big-headed, for goodness sake?

He took the conker out for a closer look.

'Glad it's already on a bootlace,' said Little Alpesh. 'That saves me a bit of trouble. Surely this isn't *really* the conker as hard as a diamond?'

He tapped it: tap-tap. It sounded like an ordinary conker.
He sniffed it: sniff-sniff. It smelled like an ordinary conker.
He licked it: lick-lick. It tasted like an ordinary conker.
Yuk!

In fact this conker was just about as ordinary as it could possibly be. It lay there, in the palm of Little Alpesh's hand, all round and brown and conkery-looking just like a midget boxing-glove with its thumb missing. In other words, it was the same as all the other conkers you've ever come across.

'How can I become Conker Champion of the Universe with this?' wailed Little Alpesh. 'It'll bust straight away like all my conkers did last year.'

Sadly, he started for home. But he was a cheerful little chap, was Alpesh, and pretty soon he was whistling as he walked and twirling the conker on the end of its string so it flashed in the Sunday sunlight.

At the park gates he met some friends of his.

'Hello, Alpesh,' they said. 'See you've found the conker as hard as a diamond!'

'That's right,' laughed Little Alpesh. 'Better keep clear of it or it'll knock you into the middle of next week – maybe as far as Friday.'

'Great!' said the kids. 'We'd miss a whole week's school, just about. See you, Alpesh.'

'See you,' called Alpesh.

And he twirled the conker harder than ever.

Now, just outside the park there happened to be an old tree – and when I say old I mean really, truly old. This tree was absolutely *historical*. For years and years and years it had been rained upon till it was completely soggy inside. Also the frost had got at it so the trunk was splintered and blotchy, and worst of all a couple of summers ago it had been struck by lightning during a terrific thunderstorm, making every branch black and powdery. Believe me, the tree was a mess. The only smart thing about it was the notice that had been put up by the Council. This said:

DANGER. KEEP OFF. THIS TREE IS AS DEAD AS A DOORKNOCKER AND SO WILL YOU BE IF IT FALLS ON YOUR BONCE.

Well, it said something like that, anyway.

'What a ponky old tree,' said Little Alpesh. 'About time the

Council got rid of it, if you ask me.'

And still whistling, still twirling his conker, he walked past. Or nearly past. For it turned out that on one of its twirls Alpesh's conker *just* managed to brush against the tree. Very, very slightly, you understand.

It was hard enough, though. Because what came next made little Alpesh jump like a jiminy cricket.

Timber!

CRASH – CLONK – BONKETY – BONK!

'Wow!' yelped Little Alpesh.

He was lucky not to be as dead as a doorknocker because he was standing up to his knees in black, battered old tree. It was spread out all around him like a full-size Do-It-Yourself tree-struck-by-lightning kit, just out of its box. Alpesh held up the conker.

'Did you do that?' he asked.

The conker swung gently to and fro on its string.

'No,' said Little Alpesh. 'No . . . you couldn't have.'

Just then –

Hee-Haw! Hee-Haw! Hee-Haw! Hee-Haw!

Everybody knows that sound. Either it's a seaside donkey having a temper-tantrum or it's the Police.

'Hello, officer,' said Little Alpesh.

The sergeant who got out of the Panda car was so gigantic and so hairy he looked like a gingery Santa Claus dressed up in a policeman's outfit.

'You all right, son?' he said.

'Fine,' said Little Alpesh. 'Er, I think it was my fault, sir. Reckon I was the one to blame – though I didn't do it on purpose, honestly.'

'Your fault? How come, son?'

'My conker.'

'What?'

'You see, it bashed against the tree just before it fell down . . .'

'Your conker?'

'That's right. I was just kind of twirling it as I passed the tree and – what's so funny, sir?'

'Your conker?'

The policeman was laughing so much now that his whole face was like a huge gingery jelly wobbling up and down.

'Tell you what, son,' he spluttered. 'You know what that makes your conker, don't you?'

'No?'

'It makes it a *one-er*! You'd better get home quick before I decide to take it into protective custody!'

'You mean put it in prison, sir?'

'Certainly, son. Powerful conker like that shouldn't be out on the loose. Threat to public order, that there conker is.'

As Little Alpesh hurried off he could hear the policeman still giggling madly.

Now, just a bit further on towards where Alpesh lived there happened to be a tumbledown house – and when I say tumbledown I mean really, truly tumbledown. The slates were falling off the roof, the windows were boarded up and on the front door was that chalk-mark which tells you the electricity people have switched off all the power. This house was in a right state! The only neat and tidy thing about it was the notice that had been put up by the Council. This said:

DANGER. KEEP OUT. THIS HOUSE IS AS DODGY AS A DINGBAT AND SO WILL YOU BE IF YOU ARE UNDER IT WHEN IT COLLAPSES.

Well, that was more or less what it said.

'What a grotty house,' said Little Alpesh. 'Really spoils the view it does. About time the council pulled it down.' And he walked past, whistling, and twirling his conker. Or nearly walked past, rather. This time the conker just *grazed* the house...

CRASH – BANG – WALLOP and TINKLE-TINKLE, too!

Little Alpesh felt as dodgy as a dingbat standing there waist-high in slates and plaster and bricks and broken glass. He hadn't got a mark on him, though, and neither had the conker. It swayed gently to and fro as he held it up.

'Did you do that?' he asked. 'No . . . no. You couldn't . . . you couldn't possibly have.'

Hee-Haw! Hee-Haw! Hee-Haw! Hee-Haw!

Yes, it was the same sergeant with the same gingerness.

'Son,' he said anxiously. 'Son – you all right?'

'Fine,' said Little Alpesh. 'But I'd better own up, sir. It was an accident, you see, but my conker –'

'Your conker?'

'It just grazed against the house and –'

Too late. Already the policeman was snorting and sneezing with laughter fit to bust his boots.

'What a right caution you are, son,' he chortled. 'That there conker of yours is enough to cause a breach of the peace, it is. I ought to run it in for obstruction, malicious damage and being an accessory before, after and during the fracas! There's only one word for your conker, son.'

'Yes, sir?'

'It's a *two-er*! Kindly move along at once before I set up a road-block all round it. Good-bye, son.'

Now, I don't want to tell you the next bit of the story. I just can't see you believing it at all. Unfortunately, it *is* what happened next so I've got to go on. Take a deep breath, then. Ready?

Right on the corner of the street where Little Alpesh lived there was this ... this ... MULTI-STOREYED CAR PARK.

It was enormous.

It was brand new.

It was what everybody needed.

Also it was a big mistake: it had been built back to front, you see, because the workmen had started with their plans upside-down. So right in front of it stood yet another notice that had been put up by the Council. This said:

DANGER. KEEP AWAY. THIS MULTI-STOREYED CAR PARK IS AS DAFT AS A DICKORY-DOCK AND SO WILL YOU BE IF YOU ARE INSIDE WHEN WE DUFF IT UP.

Well, that's the kind of thing it said, anyhow.

'What a mingy multi-storeyed car park,' said little Alpesh. 'Fancy building it back to front! Drivers wouldn't know if they were coming or going. About time the Council demolished it, in my opinion.'

And he walked past it – very nearly.

A whistle.

A twirl.

A nudge from the conker and ...

KAPOW – WOW – WOW – WOW – WOW!

Little Alpesh felt as daft as a dickory-dock standing there up to his neck in a duffed-up multi-storeyed car park. When he'd clambered free, though, he discovered once again that he hadn't got a single scratch. Nor had the conker.

Hee-Haw! Hee-Haw! Hee-Haw! Hee-Haw!

'Don't tell me, son. Don't tell me. That aforementioned conker like what is in your possession is now a *three-er!*'

But as the giant, gingery sergeant gazed over acre after acre of wreckage his laughter slowly died away. Little Alpesh didn't like the new look on his face one little bit.

'Just a minute, son,' the sergeant said. 'Let's be having a look at that there catastrophe of a conker...'

Too late.

Already Little Alpesh was round the corner, running lickety-split. I'm not surprised, are you? Wouldn't you be in a hurry to get home if it had just been proved that you really, truly owned THE CONKER AS HARD AS A DIAMOND?

Dear Mum,

This is just to say,
It was me that took
The chocolate biscuits
You were saving for your
Coffee Morning for Africa.
And it was me who borrowed
Dad's cuff-links for the disco,
And then swapped them for
A dead hedgehog.
It was also me who
Trained the budgie to
Say 'knickers' when the
Vicar came round for tea.
And I have to confess
That I've been reading
Under the bedclothes
Every night,
And falling asleep,
Every day at school.
And the reason you found
Chewing-gum all over
My bedroom sheets,
Is because I keep
A spare bit of
'Chewy' under my pillow,
In case I need it in the middle
Of the night, after I've been watching
Horror videos round at
Kevin's when his mum's out.
But in spite of all
This I am trying to be better,
And I do love you,
And think you're the best mum
In the world.

George English

Veruca in the Nut Room

Roald Dahl

Mr Wonka rushed on down the corridor. THE NUT ROOM, it said on the next door they came to.

'All right,' said Mr Wonka, 'stop here for a moment and catch your breath, and take a peek through the glass panel of this door. But don't go in! Whatever you do, don't go into THE NUT ROOM! If you go in, you'll disturb the squirrels!'

Everyone crowded around the door.

'Oh look, Grandpa, look!' cried Charlie.

'Squirrels!' shouted Veruca Salt.

'Crikey!' said Mike Teavee.

It was an amazing sight. One hundred squirrels were seated upon high stools around a large table. On the table, there were mounds and mounds of walnuts, and the squirrels were all working away like mad, shelling the walnuts at a tremendous speed.

'These squirrels are specially trained for getting the nuts out of walnuts,' Mr Wonka explained.

'Why use squirrels?' Mike Teavee asked. 'Why not use Oompa-Loompas?'

'Because,' said Mr Wonka, 'Oompa-Loompas can't get walnuts out of walnut shells in one piece. They always break them in two. Nobody except squirrels can get walnuts *whole* out of walnut shells every time. It is extremely difficult. But in my factory, I insist upon only whole walnuts. Therefore I have to have squirrels to do the job. Aren't they wonderful, the way they get those nuts out! And see how they first tap each walnut with their knuckles to be sure it's not a bad one! If it's bad, it makes a hollow sound, and they don't bother to open it. They just throw it down the rubbish chute. There!

Look! Watch that squirrel nearest to us! I think he's got a bad one now!'

They watched the little squirrel as he tapped the walnut shell with his knuckles. He cocked his head to one side, listening intently, then suddenly he threw the nut over his shoulder into a large hole in the floor.

'Hey, Mummy!' shouted Veruca Salt suddenly. 'I've decided I want a squirrel! Get me one of those squirrels!'

'Don't be silly, sweetheart,' said Mrs Salt. 'These all belong to Mr Wonka.'

'I don't care about that!' shouted Veruca. 'I want one. All I've *got* at home is two dogs and four cats and six bunny rabbits and two parakeets and three canaries and a green parrot and a turtle and a bowl of goldfish and a cage of white mice and a silly old hamster! I want a *squirrel*!'

'All right, my pet,' Mrs Salt said soothingly. 'Mummy'll get you a squirrel just as soon as she possibly can.'

'But I don't want *any* old squirrel!' Veruca shouted. 'I want a *trained* squirrel!'

At this point, Mr Salt, Veruca's father, stepped forward. 'Very well, Wonka,' he said importantly, taking out a wallet full of money, 'how much d'you want for one of these squirrels? Name your price.'

'They're not for sale,' Mr Wonka answered. 'She can't have one.'

'Who says I can't!' shouted Veruca. 'I'm going in to get myself one this very minute!'

'Don't!' said Mr Wonka quickly, but he was too late. The girl had already thrown open the door and rushed in.

The moment she entered the room, one hundred squirrels stopped what they were doing and turned their heads and stared at her with small black beady eyes.

Veruca Salt stopped also, and stared back at them. Then her gaze fell upon a pretty little squirrel sitting nearest to her at the end of the table. The squirrel was holding a walnut in its paws.

'All right,' Veruca said, 'I'll have *you*!'

She reached out her hands to grab the squirrel . . . but as she did so . . . in that first split second when her hands started to go forward, there was a sudden flash of movement in the room, like a flash of brown lightning, and every single squirrel around the table took a flying leap towards her and landed on her body.

Twenty-five of them caught hold of her right arm, and pinned it down.

Twenty-five more caught hold of her left arm, and pinned that down.

Twenty-five caught hold of her right leg and anchored it to the ground.

Twenty-*four* caught hold of her left leg.

And the one remaining squirrel (obviously the leader of them all) climbed up on to her shoulder and started tap-tap-tapping the wretched girl's head with its knuckles.

'Save her!' screamed Mrs Salt. 'Veruca! Come back! What are they *doing* to her?'

'They're testing her to see if she's a bad nut,' said Mr Wonka. 'You watch.'

Veruca struggled furiously, but the squirrels held her tight and she couldn't move. The squirrel on her shoulder went on tap-tap-tapping the side of her head with his knuckles.

Then all at once, the squirrels pulled Veruca to the ground and started carrying her across the floor.

'My goodness, she *is* a bad nut after all,' said Mr Wonka. 'Her head must have sounded quite hollow.'

Veruca kicked and screamed, but it was no use. The tiny strong paws held her tightly and she couldn't escape.

'Where are they taking her?' shrieked Mrs Salt.

'She's going where all the other bad nuts go,' said Mr Willy Wonka. 'Down the rubbish chute.'

'By golly, she *is* going down the chute!' said Mr Salt, staring through the glass door at his daughter.

'Then save her!' cried Mrs Salt.

'Too late,' said Mr Wonka. 'She's gone!'

And indeed she had.

'But where?' shrieked Mrs Salt, flapping her arms. 'What happens to the bad nuts? Where does the chute go to?'

'That *particular* chute,' Mr Wonka told her, 'runs directly into the great big main rubbish pipe which carries away all the rubbish from every part of the factory – all the floor sweepings and potato peelings and rotten cabbages and fish heads and stuff like that.'

'Who eats fish and cabbage and potatoes in *this* factory, I'd like to know?' said Mike Teavee.

'I do, of course,' answered Mr Wonka. 'You don't think *I* live on cacao beans, do you?'

'But . . . but . . . but . . .' shrieked Mrs Salt, 'where does the great big pipe go to in the end?'

'Why, to the furnace, of course,' Mr Wonka said calmly. 'To the incinerator.'

Mrs Salt opened her huge red mouth and started to scream.

'Don't worry,' said Mr Wonka, 'there's always a chance that they've decided not to light it today.'

'A *chance*!' yelled Mrs Salt. 'My darling Veruca! She'll . . . she'll . . . be sizzled like a sausage!'

'Quite right, my dear,' said Mr Salt. 'Now see here, Wonka,' he added, 'I think you've gone *just* a shade too far this time, I do indeed. My daughter may be a bit of a frump – I don't mind admitting it – but that doesn't mean you can roast her to a crisp. I'll have you know I'm extremely cross about this, I really am.'

'Oh, don't be cross, my dear sir!' said Mr Wonka, 'I expect she'll turn up again sooner or later. She may not even have gone down at all. She may be stuck in the chute just below the entrance hole, and if *that's* the case, all you'll have to do is go in and pull her up again.'

Hearing this, both Mr and Mrs Salt dashed into the Nut Room and ran over to the hole in the floor and peered in.

'Veruca!' shouted Mrs Salt. 'Are you down there!'

There was no answer.

Mrs Salt bent further forward to get a closer look. She was now kneeling right on the edge of the hole with her head down and her enormous behind sticking up in the air like a giant mushroom. It was a dangerous position to be in. She needed only one tiny little push ... one gentle nudge in the right place ... and *that* is exactly what the squirrels gave her!

Over she toppled, into the hole head first, screeching like a parrot.

'Good gracious me!' said Mr Salt, as he watched his fat wife go tumbling down the hole, '*what* a lot of rubbish there's going to be today!' He saw her disappearing into the darkness. 'What's it like down there, Angina?' he called out. He leaned further forward.

The squirrels rushed up behind him ...

'Help!' he shouted.

But he was already toppling forward, and down the chute he went, just as his wife had done before him – and his daughter.

'Oh *dear*!' cried Charlie, who was watching with the others through the door, 'what on earth's going to happen to them now?'

'I expect someone will catch them at the bottom of the chute,' said Mr Wonka.

'But what about the great fiery incinerator?' asked Charlie.

'They only light it every other day,' said Mr Wonka. 'Perhaps this is one of the days when they let it go out. You never know ... they might be lucky ...'

'Ssshh!' said Grandpa Joe. 'Listen! Here comes another song!'

From far away down the corridor came the beating of drums. Then the singing began.

'*Veruca Salt!*' sang the Oompa-Loompas.
'*Veruca Salt, the little brute,*
Has just gone down the rubbish chute,
(And as we very rightly thought
That in a case like this we ought
To see the thing completely through,
We've polished off her parents, too).
Down goes Veruca! Down the drain!
And here, perhaps, we should explain
That she will meet, as she descends,
A rather different set of friends
To those that she has left behind –
These won't be nearly so refined.
A fish head, for example, cut
This morning from a halibut.
"Hello! Good morning! How d'you do?
How nice to meet you! How are you?"
And then a little further down
A mass of others gather round:
A bacon rind, some rancid lard,
A loaf of bread gone stale and hard,
A steak that nobody could chew,
An oyster from an oyster stew,
Some liverwurst so old and grey
One smelled it from a mile away,
A rotten nut, a reeky pear,
A thing the cat left on the chair,
And lots of other things as well,
Each with a rather horrid smell.
These are Veruca's new found friends
That she will meet as she descends,
And this is the price she has to pay
For going so very far astray.
But now, my dears, we think you might
Be wondering – is it really right
That every single bit of blame

*And all the scolding and the shame
Should fall upon Veruca Salt?
Is she the only one at fault?
For though she's spoiled, and dreadfully so,
A girl can't spoil herself, you know.
Who spoiled her, then? Ah, who indeed?
Who pandered to her every need?
Who turned her into such a brat?
Who are the culprits? Who did that?
Alas! You needn't look so far
To find out who these sinners are.
They are (and this is very sad)
Her loving parents, MUM and DAD.
And that is why we're glad they fell
Into the rubbish chute as well.'*

Louella

There was a naughty girl
And a naughty girl was she,
She brought a big gorilla,
Back home to have some tea.
Her mother said, 'Louella,
What kind of boy is this?'
Louella cried and then replied.
'Just give us fish and chips.
Just give us fish and chips,
And coke and buttered bread!'
And then she went outside,
And stood upon her head.

George English

Castles in the Sand

David Henry Wilson

'That's not a very good moat.'

Jeremy James looked up from his digging, and there stood a ginger-haired, freckle-faced boy with a very superior expression on his face. His name was Timothy Smyth-Fortescue, and he lived in the big house next door to Jeremy James's. Timothy Smyth-Fortescue had everything, did everything, and he knew everything.

'It's all over the place,' said Timothy. 'Moats should be round, not all over the place.'

'I'll bet you couldn't dig a better one,' said Jeremy James.

'Oh yes I could,' said Timothy. 'That's my castle over there, and it's miles better than yours.'

'I've only just started mine,' said Jeremy James.

'Well, your moat's all crooked,' said Timothy. 'Moats should be round, not crooked.'

'I didn't want a round moat,' said Jeremy James. 'I wanted mine to be crooked.'

'Why?' said Timothy.

'Because,' said Jeremy James.

'Because what?' said Timothy.

'Because . . .' said Jeremy James, 'because round moats are old fashioned. My Daddy told me round moats are old fashioned. People don't build round moats any more.'

'You're just saying that,' said Timothy, 'because you can't build a round moat. You don't know how to.'

'Oh yes I do,' said Jeremy James.

'Go on then,' said Timothy. 'Make a round moat.'

'I won't,' said Jeremy James.

'You can't,' said Timothy. 'You come and look at my castle, and then you'll see how proper castles are built.'

'Right,' said Jeremy James, with a determined look on his face. 'You show me your rotten castle. I'll bet it's a rotten castle. I'll bet your castle isn't nearly as good as my castle's going to be. 'Cos I'm going to build the best castle *anybody's ever* built.'

By now they had reached Timothy's castle. And it wasn't a rotten castle at all. It was a very good castle. In fact it was so good that it may well have been the best castle anybody had ever built. It had a completely round moat, lots of smooth regular towers, battlements, a drawbridge. It looked just like a real castle.

'There you are,' said Timothy. '*That's* how to build a sandcastle. And I'll bet *you* couldn't build a sandcastle like that.'

'It's all right,' said Jeremy James. 'But I've seen better ones.'

'Where?' demanded Timothy.

'Places,' said Jeremy James.

'What places?' demanded Timothy.

'Well,' said Jeremy James, 'places like ... like ... the Grandmother Polly Ann...'

'The what?' said Timothy.

'The Grandmother Polly Ann. It's a hotel...'

'You mean the Grand Metropolitan,' said Timothy. 'That's where I'm staying. And I haven't seen you there.'

'No,' said Jeremy James, 'because I'm not staying there, because we didn't want to stay there. *We've* been at Mrs Gullick's, so there.'

'The Grand Metropolitan's got five stars. I'll bet Mrs Gullick hasn't got five stars,' said Timothy.

'Who cares about stars?' said Jeremy James. '*I* had two eggs and two slices of bacon for breakfast.'

'I had poached haddock,' said Timothy. 'And four slices of toast.'

'Mrs Gullick gave me a big bar of chocolate, too,' said Jeremy James.

'Chocolate's bad for your teeth,' said Timothy. 'You shouldn't eat chocolate.'

'And you shouldn't eat poach taddock,' said Jeremy James. 'Poach taddock makes people die.'

'No it doesn't,' said Timothy.

'Yes it does,' said Jeremy James. 'I know somebody who died of poach taddock.'

'Who?' asked Timothy.

'My Mummy's Great-Aunt Maud. She ate poach taddock, and they had to put her in a box and throw her away.'

The conversation would doubtless have continued, but at this moment Timothy's mother, in a swimming costume and sun-glasses, approached the sandcastle.

'Come along, Timothy,' she said, 'we're going back to the hotel now. Oh hello, Jeremy. Fancy seeing you here! Have you come with your Mummy and Daddy?'

'Yes, Mrs Smyth-Forseasick,' said Jeremy James, who always had some difficulty with Timothy's mother's name.

'Well say hello to them for me, Jeremy,' said Mrs Smyth-Fortescue.

Jeremy James was about to remind her that his name was Jeremy *James* when she suddenly said something that he found very interesting indeed.

'What a beautiful sandcastle!' she said. 'That *is* good! Did you build that all by yourself, Jeremy?'

'No,' said Jeremy James, 'I didn't build it at all. Timothy built it.'

'Timothy,' said Mrs Smyth-Fortescue, 'did you tell Jeremy that *you* built it?'

Timothy's face went red, and he looked down at his right foot which was burying itself as deep as possible in the sand.

'You mustn't say things like that, dear,' said Mrs Smyth-Fortescue. 'It's very naughty to tell lies. Come along now, perhaps you can play with Jeremy again this afternoon. Say goodbye, dear.'

'G'bye,' said Timothy, still studying his right foot.

'G'bye,' said Jeremy James. 'Hope you have poach taddock for lunch.'

Off went Timothy with his mother, and Jeremy James returned to his crooked moat. Perhaps his sandcastle wouldn't be quite the best anybody had ever built, but at least it would be his. Jeremy James gave a cheerful smile, and began to dig.

Girl's Song
(Or things I want to be when I grow up)

I want to be a lorry driver
And always wear greasy dungarees,
I want to be an explorer,
And roam the desert at my ease,
I want to climb Mount Everest,
And chase Tarzan through the trees.

I want to be a surgeon,
Who can operate on brains,
Or work the city sewers,
And go splashing down the drains,
I want to drive a racing car
And pilot aeroplanes.

I want to be more than the girl,
Who's always wearing whites,
Who's always playing weddings,
And is dressed in silvery tights,
I want to run the darkened streets,
Alone on wintry nights.

I want to be the kind of girl,
Who's busy everywhere,
Who fights the boys
And blacks their eyes,
And sees the way they scare,
Then turns her head and laughs out loud,
A girl without a care.

George English

Temper, Temper...

Jules Older

One day Henrietta's temper proved too great even for Mrs Kapa, her teacher, who was the very picture of patience.

'Henrietta,' she said, 'I'm the very picture of patience, but your temper has proved too great even for me.'

Henrietta glared up from her desk, 'I didn't do nuffin'.'

'Henrietta, I didn't do *anything*.'

'I never said you did.'

Mrs Kapa looked confused. 'Never said I did what, Henrietta?'

'I never said you did anything. It's you who's been pickin' on me all day.'

'Henrietta, that's the last straw.'

'I don't care!'

'You're going to write, "I will not lose my temper in class," five hundred times.'

'I WON'T!'

'You won't what, Henrietta?' Mrs Kapa suddenly looked very big and scary as she loomed over Henrietta's desk.

'I ... WON'T ... lose my temper in class, Mrs Kapa.'

'Indeed, you won't, my girl. And I want five hundred lines to that effect by tomorrow morning.'

Henrietta stopped talking, but she didn't stop thinking. It's not fair, she thought. It's not fair at all. So what if I have a bad temper. Toby's rude, but Mrs Kapa doesn't make him write, 'I won't be rude in class.' Laura has red hair, but she doesn't have to write, 'I won't be a redhead in class.' Well, I've got a temper. But I'm not gonna write any five hundred lines about it. It's just not fair.

Henrietta kept on thinking, and by three o'clock, Henrietta had a plan. As soon as the bell rang, she ran out of

class and down the hall to the front door. When the other kids came tumbling out of their classrooms and spilling out of the door, she hauled out her friends as they passed. First Laura, then Toby and Sandeep, and finally Natalie and Ben. When she had them all assembled, here's what she said:

'Look you guys, we've got a problem. Mrs Kapa told me I had to write five hundred lines by tomorrow morning.'

'Then why do *we* have a problem?' Toby wanted to know.

'Because *we* know it's not fair that *I* have to write five hundred lines.'

'You probably deserved it,' Toby answered. He liked Mrs Kapa a lot.

'You shut up, Toby,' Henrietta snapped back. 'I need your help. Five hundred lines is a lot, but if we each write one hundred, I could hand them in tomorrow, and she'd never know the difference. So we each go home and write one hundred times, "I will not lose my temper in class."'

Toby piped up again. 'Wait a minute. There's five of us, not counting you, Henrietta. If all of us do one hundred lines, then you don't have to do any. Besides, you probably deserved it – so count me out!'

Henrietta glared at him as he ran off, but the others stayed and copied down the sentence. They all agreed to deliver one hundred lines apiece to Henrietta before nine o'clock the next morning.

That night Henrietta wrote, 'I will not lose my temper in class,' one hundred times in her exercise book, then carefully tore the page out of the book. She went to bed chuckling about how clever she was.

The next morning she got up early and waited for her friends just outside the school door. They straggled into school, one by one.

Sandeep was first to arrive. He handed her his one hundred lines carefully written on exercise paper with black ink. Then Laura rode up on her bike and gave Henrietta one hundred lines written on a writing pad with blue ink. Ben's one hundred lines were on school paper like Henrietta's, but he had scribbled them in pencil. Natalie's contribution was beautifully printed on Holly Hobby stationery. All her i's were dotted with hearts.

Henrietta handed all five pages to Mrs Kapa. Mrs Kapa looked at Henrietta's page and smiled. Then Mrs Kapa looked at Sandeep's page and smiled a little less. Then Mrs Kapa looked at Ben's page with puzzled eyes. Then Mrs Kapa considered Laura's page. And finally, Mrs Kapa carefully examined Natalie's page with all the i's dotted with hearts.

'Henrietta,' she sighed, 'did you do all these lines yourself?'

Henrietta's temper ripped into top gear. 'You never said I had to do them myself. You just said I had to GET THEM DONE!'

'Oh,' replied Mrs Kapa calmly. 'Well, perhaps I didn't specify that you were to do them yourself, Henrietta. I'm so sorry. Tonight you can write five hundred more lines, and this time, please do them yourself.'

Henrietta was about to hit the roof when she noticed that Mrs Kapa was looking unnaturally calm. She looked the kind of calm teachers look before they blow up and yell for the principal and start throwing erasers around the room. Henrietta said nothing.

But Henrietta kept on thinking. After school that day, Henrietta went straight home to her parents' desk. She knew just what she was looking for. She opened the stationery drawer and pulled out nine pieces of paper. Five of them were white typing paper and four were black carbon paper. She laid one white sheet on the desk and placed one black sheet of carbon paper neatly on top of it. On top of that she put one more piece of white, and on top of that, one more piece of carbon. When they were all carefully stacked and a fresh, clean sheet of white paper rested on the top as well as the bottom, Henrietta took out a ballpoint. As hard as she could, she wrote on the top sheet, 'I will not lose my temper in class.' She wrote it one hundred times. Then she carefully lifted the four sheets of carbon paper from the pile. On every white sheet the words, 'I will not lose my temper in class,' appeared one hundred times. Henrietta looked very satisfied with herself. 'Hummph,' she muttered, 'hot-tempered I may be, but dumb I'm not.'

Next morning Henrietta handed Mrs Kapa the five sheets of paper, each with the same sentence written one hundred times.

'This time I did them myself!'

Mrs Kapa looked at the first sheet and smiled. Mrs Kapa then looked at the second sheet and smiled a little less. Mrs Kapa looked at the third sheet with puzzled eyes. Mrs Kapa frowned as she studied the fourth sheet. When she examined the fifth sheet, Mrs Kapa grew very quiet. 'Henrietta,' she said at last, 'I don't think you wrote these yourself.'

Henrietta's temper shot up like a rocket. 'I didn't say I *wrote* them myself! I said I *did* them myself. That's what you told me to do, AND THAT'S WHAT I DID!'

'Henrietta, what was that sentence I gave you to wri— to do?'

'I WILL NOT LOSE MY TEMPER IN CLASS!'

'And what are you doing now, Henrietta?'

'I AM NOT LOSING MY...'

'Yes, Henrietta, you are not losing your...?'

Now a puzzled look crept into *Henrietta's* eyes.

Mrs Kapa smiled. 'Henrietta,' she said, 'if I told you to do those five hundred lines again tonight, I suppose you'd photocopy them.'

'Well...'

'Well, what, Henrietta?'

'Well,' Henrietta answered slowly, 'there's a Xerox machine where my Dad works...'

'And if I said to do them again tomorrow night?'

Henrietta smiled. 'Sandeep has a computer, Mrs Kapa.'

Now Mrs Kapa smiled. 'Henrietta, you really must learn to control your temper in class. It gets you in trouble too much of the time.'

Henrietta felt another burst of temper coming on right then.

Mrs Kapa went on. 'Yes, Henrietta, you must learn to control your temper, but I'm not sure that writing lines is going to help you do it. You're obviously a good thinker. So the next time you feel a temper coming on, try to think before you explode.'

Henrietta thought.

Henrietta smiled.

Henrietta walked over to her desk and sat down.

There Was a Young Girl from Asturias

There was a young girl from Asturias
Whose temper was frantic and furious.
She used to throw eggs
At her Grandmother's legs –
A habit unpleasant, but curious.

Anon.

In the Larder

MARION ST JOHN WEBB

As Mr Papingay bustled back into the parlour he turned to Robin and said: 'I am a little anxious about the Greedy Boy. He's been quiet this long while, so he's sure to be in some mischief. Would you mind going down and finding him – and, whatever he's doing – tell him not to do it. Thank you. Thank you very much indeed.'

So Robin went down the stairs into the basement, and along a narrow, dark passage with a lighted door at the end that had 'LARDER' painted on it in black letters.

As he neared the door it opened slowly and a face peered cautiously round the side. It was a greedy face, a very greedy face indeed, and the owner had tiny eyes that kept blinking, and a lot of red hair on his head.

Robin stood still and looked at the face of the Greedy Boy; and the Greedy Boy blinked back at him, then said in a thick, husky voice:

'Oh, it's only you, is it? I thought it was *her*,' and he made a disagreeable squeaky noise, and screwed up one eye.

'Her?' said Robin.

'Miss Penny,' explained the Greedy Boy. 'I thought she'd come to measure the butter with a tape-measure, or count the jam tarts again! ... She says I'm always eating her cakes.' He gave a chuckle, then added, 'And of course, I am! What's the good of being called a greedy pig if you aren't a greedy pig? You might just as well *be* one!'

Robin thought this over for a moment.

'Oh, but –' he began, but the Greedy Boy interrupted him.

'Here – you come and look here,' he beckoned. So Robin went inside the larder.

Spread out on the shelves were a number of plates and dishes full of tempting cakes and fruit and puddings and chocolates.

'Oh–h!' breathed Robin, his eyes opening wide. 'Are they giving a party?'

'Umps,' said the Greedy Boy, running his finger round the edge of a bowl of cream, then putting it in his mouth. 'That tastes good . . . I'm supposed to be cleaning the spoons, ready for the party – but I thought I'd just look in here to see that the mice hadn't got in!' He helped himself to a jam puff. 'Mice!' he said, and gave a hoarse laugh. 'Oh, the mice do eat up the things in here something shocking!'

Robin watched with dismay as the Greedy Boy picked out a dainty pink iced cake and began to stuff it into his mouth.

'Mice! That's what I tell *her*.' The Greedy Boy grinned and made the disagreeable squeaky noise again and screwed up his eye.

'Oh, you mustn't!' protested Robin. 'If – if you go on like that there won't be any party. Besides, I've been sent down to tell you –'

The Greedy Boy set to work on a big raspberry tart.

'I'm the party,' he chortled with his mouth full.

Robin hesitated, not knowing what to do. It seemed sneaky to go and tell on the Greedy Boy, and yet –

'I've been sent down to tell you –' he began again; but the Greedy Boy wasn't listening.

'When I go to bed at night and dream about food – I like that,' said the Greedy Boy. 'Then I get all my meals twice over, as you might say.' Suddenly he began to sing, stopping every few lines to take another mouthful of tart:

> 'I like a dream that is full of eating –
> Cakes, and puddings, and pies.
> Raspberry pies want a lot of beating;
> Pies of enormous size!
>   Me – *very little*.
>   The pie – VERY BIG.
> Pick up a fork and into it dig.
> Eat a bit, dig a bit, eat a bit more,
> Never such pie have I tasted before!
>   Crispy and brown,
>   Gollop it down –'

('He really is a greedy pig,' thought Robin to himself.)

> 'And when it's all eaten – the very last lump,
> Lay down the fork and the spoon with a thump!
> And wake up, and get up, and start eating quick,
> For dream-time'll come round again in a tick!'

The Greedy Boy gave a sigh as he peered into the empty pie-dish. 'I think that's a nice song I just sung you,' he said, laying down his spoon. 'And that was a nice pie I just eat up too. I wish there was some more.'

His eyes roved round the shelves while he considered what he should eat next.

'Look here —' Robin began, but stopped as the Greedy Boy held up a warning finger, and whispered 'Sh!'

A creaking sound could be heard on the basement stairs. Quickly the Greedy Boy hid the empty pie-dish. 'It's *her*,' he said, and in a faint voice repeated the disagreeable, squeaky noise, and screwed up one eye.

'What are you doing in the larder?' came Penny's voice.

'Only showing Master Robin the party things, and putting the clean forks away,' answered the Greedy Boy.

Penny appeared in the doorway. She looked at Robin. She looked at the Greedy Boy. She said nothing, but took a piece of chalk from a little bag she carried, and chalked in large figures '97' on the larder door.

Then taking Robin by the hand she led him upstairs, leaving the Greedy Boy twisting a corner of his apron round and round and staring at the white chalk mark.

'She's done it afore,' Robin could hear him muttering. 'Counting up the times she's caught me in the larder, I suppose ... I wonder what she'll do when it gets to one hundred!'

To Market to Market

To market to market
With my brother Jim
Somebody threw a tomato at him
Tomatoes are soft and they don't hurt the skin
But this one was hard and it came in a tin.

Anon.

The Secret

Gene Kemp

After school I went to play with the kitten, then sat on the stile and thought about it and about being good. I'd got all my spellings right that day. Anyone who could get all their spellings right could be good for long enough to have a kitten when it was old enough, I thought.

Tom ran down the path, jumped over the stile, just missing me, and then sat down on the top bar.

'I've found a secret place,' he told me. 'Only it's a long way away and you're not to tell anyone. Especially Evie. You always tell her things.'

'No I don't.'

'Yes you do. You forget and tell her secrets.'

'NO I DON'T, NO I DON'T.'

'Shut up. And don't cry. You don't want to be called a cry-baby. Here, I've got one sweet left. You can have it.'

After a while I asked, 'Where's this secret place?'

'A long way away. Too far to go after school so I'll take you when we break up.'

'Break up what?'

'School, stupid.'

'It's not me that's stupid. It's stupid to say break up school. We don't knock it to bits at the end of each term. Besides, Evie says I'm clever.'

'So. Evie's stupid.'

'She's a teacher!'

'So. Teachers are stupid.'

'You're horrible, our Tom.'

'Anybody horrible wouldn't tell you two secrets in one go.'

'You've only told me one.'

'Here's the other one. Evie's got two big Easter eggs in her

case under the bed. And one has got purple sugar violets on it.'

'PURPLE SUGAR VIOLETS!'

'Pipe down, Annie. Somebody will hear.'

'Let's go and have a look.'

'No, not now. We'll have to wait till they're out, and then creep up. But don't tell anybody. Promise.'

'Cross my heart and hope to die.'

'I'm off now.'

'Let me come. Please.'

'No.' He walked away whistling.

I stayed on the stile. I tried to think about my kitten. I tried to think about the dragon in the well. I tried to think about the new dress my mother was making me for Easter.

But all I could think about was the big chocolate Easter egg with purple sugar violets on it. Would there be green leaves as well? You could pick the violets off one at a time and suck them. Though I wouldn't do that. I'd just hold the Easter egg and look at it.

I went back in the house. It was very quiet, nobody about. The kettle was singing on the black hob of the grate and Blackie was asleep on the hearthrug.

I called my mother softly. No one answered. It was very quiet. I called Evie very softly. No one answered. I could hear myself breathing. What would happen if I stopped breathing? I'd be dead. It must be funny to be dead.

I started to go up the stairs, softly, softly, though what did it matter if I was caught going upstairs? I was going to get something from the chair at the side of my bed. A book. I was going to get a book from the chair at the side of my bed. A door creaked and I stopped dead like in playing Creeping Up. Then it was quiet again.

The big room was where Polly and Evie and Nell slept. I tiptoed on Polly's rugs over to the window where Evie's bed was. Her bedcover was blue, Polly's gold, and Nell's green. I liked going into their room and looking at their things, but I wasn't supposed to if no one was there.

I knelt down by Evie's bed and lifted up the cover. If anyone came in I'd say I was looking for ... for ... my handkerchief. There was Evie's blue case. I pulled it towards me and slowly lifted up the lid ...

And there they were. In the case. Just as Tom said they were. Wrapped in cellophane.

One chocolate Easter egg had green leaves and red roses on it, and the other – the other – with trembling hands I reached out to touch it – had green leaves and PURPLE SUGAR VIOLETS!!!

OH!!!

The lid dropped down. I pulled out my fingers just in time.

'And just what do you think you're doing?' asked Evie.

I lay in bed. Outside it had started to rain. You could hear it on the windows. I was not Happy.

Tom came in and shut the door quietly.

'What did you have to go and do a daft thing like that for? I told you to wait. Instead you've gone and mucked it all up and they say we shan't have the eggs now. Here, wipe your eyes with this.'

'But you told me. You told me they were there. You did.'

'I didn't tell you to go poking around looking for them.'

'I'll tell Evie you said they were there, so you must've looked as well.'

'Do that and I shan't take you to that secret place.'

'Tom Sutton, it's not fair. You're not fair.'

He grinned at me and whistled and I was full of anger so that it lifted me out of the bed and across the room and I jumped at him and scratched him hard on his forehead and it bled...

Everywhere just as Evie and my mother and Polly all walked into the room and he, that Tom Sutton, showed them his head, and said that I did it, and I hid under the bedclothes and cried for I knew there wouldn't be any Easter egg, no secret place, no kitten, not for me, not now...

Micky

Micky didn't mind
When they left him far behind.
Left him standing there,
To linger by the pond and stare
At swans sedate upon a mirror
Of green glass.
Slowly they were blown to him,
Silently he watched them pass.

He could have stayed all day,
All day staring at the swans,
Then somebody saw they'd lost him,
Then they found him by the pond.

Now back at home,
They have sent him to his room
For staying there,
There beside the swans,
Yet staring at the wall he doesn't care,
For he can see them far beyond,
The white sails gliding on the pond,
Forever near him, forever far beyond.

George English

When Emil Got His Head Stuck in the Soup Tureen

Astrid Lindgren

That day they were having meat broth for dinner in Katthult. Lina had served it up in the flowered soup tureen and they were all sitting round the kitchen table eating soup. Emil especially liked soup; you could hear that when he ate it.

'Must you make that noise?' asked his mother.

'Well, you can't tell you're having soup, otherwise,' said Emil.

Everyone had as much as they wanted, and the tureen was empty except for a tiny little drop left at the bottom. But Emil wanted that little drop, and the only way he could get it was by pushing his head into the tureen and sucking it up. And that is just what he did. But just fancy! When he tried to get his head out again he *couldn't*! He was stuck fast. It frightened him and he jumped up from the table and stood there with the tureen like a tub on his head. It came right down over his eyes and ears. He hit at it and screamed. Lina was very upset.

'Our lovely soup tureen,' she said. 'Our lovely bowl with the flowers on it. Whatever shall we put the soup in now?'

Because although she wasn't very bright, she did realize that while Emil was in the tureen it would be impossible to serve soup in it.

Emil's mother, however, was more worried about Emil.

'Dear sake's alive, how shall we get the child out? We'll have to get the poker and break the bowl.'

'Have you taken leave of your senses?' asked Emil's father. 'That bowl cost four kronor!'

'Let me have a try,' said Alfred, who was a strong, hefty farm-hand. He took hold of both handles and lifted the tureen high up in the air – but what good was that? Emil went with it. Because he was stuck really tight. And there he hung, kicking, trying to get back on the ground again.

'Let go! Let me get down! Let go, I tell you!' he yelled. So Alfred did let go.

Now everybody was very upset. They stood in the kitchen in a ring round Emil, wondering what to do – father Anton, mother Alma, little Ida, Alfred and Lina. Nobody could think of a good way of getting Emil out of the soup tureen.

'Look, Emil's crying!' said little Ida, pointing at two big tears sliding down Emil's cheeks from under the edge of the tureen.

'No I'm not,' said Emil. 'It's soup.'

He sounded as cocky as ever, but it isn't much fun being stuck inside a soup tureen – and supposing he never managed to get out! Poor Emil, when would he be able to wear his cap then?

Emil's mother was in great distress about her little boy. She wanted to take the poker and break the tureen, but his father said, 'Not on any account! That bowl cost four kronor. We had better go to the doctor in Mariannelund. He'll be able to get it off. He'll only charge three kronor, and we'll save a krona that way.'

Emil's mother thought that a good idea. It isn't every day that one can save a whole krona. Think of all the nice things you could buy with that: perhaps something for little Ida, who would have to stay at home while Emil was out enjoying the trip.

Now all was hurry and bustle in Katthult. Emil must be made tidy, he must be washed and dressed in his best clothes. He couldn't have his hair combed, of course, and nobody could wash his ears, although they certainly needed washing. His mother did try to get her finger under the rim of the soup tureen so as to get at one of Emil's ears, but that wasn't much use for she, too, got stuck in the bowl.

'There now!' said little Ida, and father Anton got really angry, though as a rule he was very good-tempered.

'Does anyone else want to get stuck in the tureen?' he shouted. 'Well, get on with it for goodness' sake, and I'll bring out the big hay wagon and take everyone in the house over to the doctor in Mariannelund.'

But Emil's mother wriggled her finger and managed to get it out. 'You'll have to go without washing your ears, Emil,' she said, blowing her finger. A pleased smile could be seen under the rim of the tureen, and Emil said, 'That's the first bit of luck I've had from this tureen.'

Alfred had brought the horse and trap to the front steps and Emil now came out to climb into the trap. He was very smart in his striped Sunday suit and black button boots and the soup tureen – of course it did look a trifle unusual, but it was gay and flowery, something like a new-fashioned summer hat. The only criticism that might have been made was that it came down rather too far over Emil's eyes.

Then they set off for Mariannelund.

'Be sure to look after little Ida properly while we're away,' called Emil's mother. She sat in front with Emil's father. Emil and the tureen sat at the back, and Emil had his cap beside him on the seat. Because of course he would need something to put on his head for the journey back home. A good job he remembered that!

'What shall I get ready for supper?' shouted Lina, just as the trap was moving off.

'Anything you like,' called back Emil's mother. 'I've other things to think about just now.'

'Well, I'll make meat broth then,' said Lina. But at that moment she saw something flowery disappearing round the corner of the road and remembered what had happened. She turned sadly back to Alfred and little Ida.

'It'll have to be black pudding and pork, instead,' she said.

Emil had been several times to Mariannelund. He used to like sitting high up in the trap, watching the winding road and looking at the farms they passed on the way, and the children who lived in them, and the dogs that barked at the gates, and the horses and cows grazing in the meadows. But now it was hardly any fun at all. He sat with a soup tureen over his eyes and could only see a little bit of his own button boots from under the tightly fitting rim of the tureen. He had to keep on asking his father, 'Where are we now? Have we got to the pancake place yet? Are we nearly at the pig place?'

Emil had got his own names for all the farms along the road. The pancake place was so-called because of two small, fat children who had once stood by the gate eating pancakes as Emil went past. And the pig place owed its name to a jolly pig whose back Emil would scratch sometimes.

But now he sat gloomily looking down at his own button boots, unable to see either pancakes or jolly little pigs. Small wonder that he kept whining, 'Where are we now? Are we nearly at Mariannelund?'

The doctor's waiting-room was full of people when Emil

and the tureen went striding in. Everybody there was very sorry for him. They realized that an accident had happened. All except one horrid old man who laughed like anything, just as though there was something funny about being stuck in a soup tureen.

'Haha! Haha!' said the old man. 'Are your ears cold, my boy?'

'No,' said Emil.

'Well, why are you wearing that contraption, then?' asked the old man.

'Because otherwise my ears *would* be cold,' said Emil. He too could be funny if he liked, although he was so young.

Then it was his turn to go in and see the doctor, and the doctor didn't laugh at him.

He just said, 'Good morning! What are you doing in there?'

Emil couldn't see the doctor, but in spite of that of course he had to greet him, so he bowed as low as he could, tureen and all. Crash! went the tureen, and there it lay, broken in two. For Emil's head had banged against the doctor's desk.

'There goes four kronor up in smoke,' said Emil's father to his mother, in a low voice. But the doctor heard him.

'Yes, it's saved you a krona,' he said. 'Because I generally charge five kronor for getting small boys out of soup tureens, and he's managed to do it all by himself.'

There Was a Young Boy from Porthcawl

There was a young boy from Porthcawl
Who went to a fancy dress ball.
   He went just for fun
   Dressed up as a bun,
And a dog ate him up in the hall.

Anon.

Marmalade and Rufus at the Ritz

Andrew Davies

The Ritz Hotel is one of the poshest hotels in London, and not used to bad girls and scruffy donkeys. The reason why Marmalade told the policeman she was going to the Ritz was that it was the only hotel in London she could remember the name of. Her father had often mentioned it. When he went down to London to sell things to Sheikhs, he often met them for tea at the Ritz. (The Sheikhs would pay the bill.) The Ritz is a very nice place to be, except when it comes to paying the bill. The cream cakes are the creamiest in the world, the steaks are the juiciest in the world, and the beds are the softest in the world. But if you ever go to the Ritz, *make sure someone else is paying the bill*.

Mr Atkins always made sure that someone else was paying the bill. On one occasion the Sheikhs didn't turn up, and after Mr Atkins had eaten sixteen cucumber sandwiches and seven cream cakes, the waiter brought him the bill. It cost so much that Mr Atkins decided he would have to do a Mad Dog. Doing a Mad Dog means running out of a restaurant very fast when they bring the bill, howling at the top of your voice. It usually works if you run fast enough, but you can only get away with it once in each place, unless you go back in disguise. Doing a Mad Dog is also against the law, and even Mr Atkins, who was a bit of a crook, would only do Mad Dogs in extreme emergencies. But he was fond of the Ritz Hotel, even though he always had to wear a false moustache when he went for tea there, and this was how Marmalade and Rufus found themselves walking up the steps to the main entrance.

At the top of the steps stood an enormous doorman in a large peaked cap and a uniform so thickly decorated with medal ribbons and festooned with gold braid he looked like a cross between a Christmas tree and the survivor of a spaghetti fight.

'Evening, cock,' said Marmalade. 'Don't tell me, I know – you went to a party as a Christmas tree and someone pelted you with spaghetti!'

The doorman turned crimson and his eyes bulged like lollipops. 'I am the Head Doorman at the Ritz,' he said, 'and you are a rude little girl. The rules here are no jeans and no donkeys. Kindly leave the premises, or you'll feel the toe of my shiny black boot!'

Marmalade thought quickly. 'Just my little joke, cock,' she said. 'And you've got it all wrong. My friend and I are eccentric millionaires, and *we've* just come back from a fancy dress party. I went as Marmalade Atkins, and my friend here went as a donkey.'

'Hee haw,' said Rufus affably.

The doorman looked at them suspiciously. It didn't sound a very likely tale, but then some millionaires *are* very eccentric, and if he booted two real millionaires down the steps he might lose his job and have to hand in his lovely uniform.

'May I enquire your names?' he said.

'Certainly, cock,' said Marmalade, trying to keep a straight face. 'I'm Lord Pratt and he's Lord Spratt.'

The Head Doorman gasped. Lords as well as millionaires! He decided to give them the benefit of the doubt.

'Please proceed to Reception, my Lords,' he said, and stood aside. Marmalade and Rufus went through into the Grand Reception Hall and the Head Doorman watched them go, scratching his head and hoping he had made the right decision. Seen from the back, Lord Spratt's donkey costume was incredibly realistic.

'How can we help you?' said the Reception Clerk.

'Lord Pratt and Lord Spratt,' said Marmalade. 'We've come for a jolly good nosh-up, and then we want a bed for the

night. Big one for him, small one for me.'

'Very difficult, my lord,' said the Reception Clerk. 'The Ritz is chock-a-block tonight. A whole gang of millionaires just jetted in on Concorde, and we have only one suite left. But it's a very nice one, my lord.'

'How much does it cost?' said Marmalade.

'Five hundred pounds a night,' said the Reception Clerk. 'It's very luxurious, though. We call it the Golden Fleece Suite, my lord, all the fittings are solid gold.'

'Sounds all right, cock,' said Marmalade. 'Bit on the dear side, though. How about a little reduction, I mean if we made our own beds and that?'

'Ah, what sort of sum did you have in mind, sir?' said the Reception Clerk, fingering the carnation in his buttonhole.

Marmalade counted the pennies in the battered straw hat. 'How about forty-three pence?' she said.

The Reception Clerk let out a short uneasy giggle. 'My lord enjoys his little joke,' he said. 'Perhaps you have a credit card, sir? American Express? Diners Club?'

Marmalade searched the back pocket of her jeans.

'I've got this,' she said, and pushed a grubby square of cardboard across the gleaming desk. Wrinkling his nose in distaste, the Reception Clerk picked it up between finger and thumb, and read what it said. On the front was:

LURNATROT PONY AND GYMKHANA CLUB
This is to certify that
MARMALADE ATKINS
is a member of this club

On the back it said:

This member is
EXPELLED FROM THE CLUB
and
BANNED FOR LIFE.

The Reception Clerk raised his eyes from the card and took his first really good look at Lord Pratt and Lord Spratt. What he saw made him close the hotel register with a loud bang.

'You are not millionaires at all,' he said icily. 'You are simply a pair of oiks and down-and-outs trying to take us for a ride! Kindly leave at once!'

'Tell you what,' said Marmalade. 'You let us stay here and we *will* take you for a ride, how about that?'

'Out,' said the Reception Clerk.

'Aw, come on, cock. You've got food and we're hungry, you've got beds and we're tired. We'd pay you back some day, honest. You wouldn't see us starve, would you?'

I suppose there *was* just a slim chance that the Reception Clerk might have chosen Marmalade and Rufus for his good deed of the year, but just at that moment Rufus, who was very peckish after his dance routine, leaned over the counter, pulled the carnation out of the clerk's buttonhole, and ate it.

'That does it!' screamed the Reception Clerk. 'Out this moment, the pair of you, or I'll call the police!'

'Keep your hair on, cock,' said Marmalade. 'Come, Rufus. We shall take our custom elsewhere.'

Rufus was rather reluctant to go; he had enjoyed the carnation, and by the time Marmalade had got him out, he had eaten two flower arrangements, half a potted palm, and most of the gold braid off the doorman's epaulettes. The doorman did his level best to kick Marmalade and Rufus down the steps, but a doorman is not an even match for a donkey in a kicking match. The doorman had first go, but Rufus did a little sideways shuffle and the doorman's shiny black boot went through a plate-glass window. Then it was Rufus's turn, and the doorman found himself whizzing round and round in the revolving doors like a spinning top.

'We'll be back!' yelled Marmalade, as they stood on the chilly dark pavement outside. She said it in a loud, bold, confident way, but really she had no idea how she could make a come-back at the Ritz Hotel, and what was more she was tired and hungry and she didn't know where to lay her head for the night.

'Oh, Rufus, cock,' she said, 'what are we going to do now?'

Rufus jerked his shaggy old head towards a little alley that led round the side of the Ritz Hotel.

'Round the back,' he said. 'Never seen a fence as didn't have no gap in it.'

The back of the Ritz Hotel was quite different from the front. It was dark and dingy and cold as a medieval castle, with padlocked doors and bars over the windows. No chance at all of getting in. Marmalade saw a row of big cardboard boxes that had once held smoked salmon and caviare and other posh foods.

'Come on, Rufus,' she said. 'We could make ourselves a shelter out of them.'

But when she lifted the flap of the first box an aggrieved voice shouted: 'Find your own box, Sonny Jim! This one's mine, so it is!' Marmalade could just make out a pair of bloodshot eyes staring out of a whiskery face. The box was a tramp's bedroom. It was the same with all the boxes. All full of tramps and down-and-outs, some chewing on bones, some smoking dog-ends, some snoring away like steam engines.

Marmalade and Rufus sat down on a grating, where the warm air coming up from the kitchen below could take the chill off their bottoms.

'Think we'll have to stay here all night?' said Marmalade.

'Something'll turn up, I dare say,' said Rufus. 'Something mostly does.'

And just then, something did. The kitchen door flew open and a voice yelled up from the basement: 'Two extra washers up needed in the kitchen. First two down the steps get the job!'

All the tramps and down-and-outs started clambering out of their boxes, and the reek of old smoked salmon and stale caviare filled the air. But Marmalade and Rufus had a head start on them and were down the steps and through the door in a flash.

'Two washers up reporting for duty, sir,' said Marmalade. Luckily it was so steamy and smoky in the kitchen that the Head Chef didn't notice anything unusual about his two new employees.

'Lotsa work for you tonight, boys,' he said. 'We gotta bigga party in tonight. Aristotle Carioutabotl and all his friends just flown in onna Concorde, havea bigga banquet, see how they usea all the plates up!'

He pointed, and through the steam Marmalade could make out a giant sink in the corner with a pile of plates in it reaching to the ceiling. There were more piles of plates by the side of the sink, and gangs of waiters were crashing in through the swing-doors bringing even more plates. It was a washer-up's nightmare.

'Leave it to us, cock,' said Marmalade. 'We'll sort it out for you!'

'Thatsa good boys,' said the Head Chef. 'Aprons over there, mops in the sink!'

Marmalade and Rufus got into their aprons (Marmalade's was about six sizes too big and Rufus's was about six sizes too small) and they got to work. It was a bit of a problem. The sink was so high that Marmalade could hardly see over the top of it. Rufus could, if he stood on his hind legs, but he wasn't used to holding a mop in his hooves, and tended to drop the plates on the floor. In the end, Rufus stood by the sink, and Marmalade sat on his back to wash the dishes, drying them on Rufus's apron. Rufus obligingly wiggled his backside to help with the drying, but as the apron didn't quite cover him, quite a few shaggy ginger hairs got on to the plates.

And what was worse, no matter how hard they worked,

they still couldn't keep up. More and more waiters came crashing through the swing-doors with more and more plates, many of them loaded with disgusting leftovers that had to be scraped into the bin. It was ten times worse than school dinners at the Convent, thought Marmalade to herself. Sister Purification and Sister Conception would have something to say if they saw all this carry on. They'd rant and shout and put themselves about all right . . . Marmalade stopped, and hit herself on the head with the mop. Of course. If *they* could put themselves about at school dinners, why shouldn't *she* put herself about in the dining-room of the Ritz?

'Come on, Rufus,' she said. 'Let's get amongst 'em!'

'Thought you'd never say it,' grunted Rufus, and with Marmalade still on his back, he charged through the swing-doors, knocking over two waiters who were on their way in.

'Stop! Stop!' yelled the Head Chef. 'You canta go in there!' But it was too late. They were in.

Aristotle Carioutabotl was one of the richest men in the world. He owned about forty-four oil tanker ships, and he went about doing exactly what he liked. What he liked best of all was jetting about on Concorde and holding huge banquets at posh hotels with all his not-quite-so-rich friends. He had terrible table manners. He spoke with his mouth full, he put his elbows on the table, he took food off other people's plates, he left lots of disgusting leftovers on his own plate, and he tended to throw bread rolls at the waiters. And he was doing all these things when Rufus crashed through the swing-doors with Marmalade Atkins on his back, and skidded to a halt on the marble floor of the Ritz dining-room.

He was so astonished at the sight of Marmalade and Rufus in their aprons and cooks' hats that he stopped throwing bread at the waiters and stared at Marmalade, licking gravy off his gold and diamond rings, unable for the moment to think what to say.

'Which one of you lot is Aristotle Carioutabotl?' said Marmalade.

'I am,' said Aristotle Carioutabotl, speaking as usual with his mouth full, and spraying the nearest ten people with gravy. 'What's this – the cabaret?'

Marmalade summoned up her best Sister Purification voice. 'You,' she said, 'are a disgusting little millionaire! How dare you speak to me with your mouth full? I am not angry. I am not upset. I am just very, very disappointed. I have never seen such disgusting behaviour at school dinners, and you are all going to be very very sorry. Especially you, Aristotle Carioutabotl!'

A deep silence fell on the Ritz dining-room. All the rich jet-setters held their breath and waited to see what Aristotle Carioutabotl would do to Marmalade Atkins. He was famous for his rages and his mad rampages.

But Aristotle Carioutabotl just sat and stared at Marmalade with his mouth wide open. Everyone could see the horrible half-chewed pheasant and venison and truffles and the glitter of his solid gold teeth. The manager rushed up to him anxiously: 'Terribly sorry, Mr Carioutabotl. I'll have them thrown out immediately!'

Then Aristotle Carioutabotl found his voice at last. 'No, no,' he said indistinctly. 'Let them stay. Never have I been spoken to like that since I was a little boy, and had a strict English Nanny. Oh, how she would tell me off and scold me! Oh, how I loved her! Oh, how I miss her! Nobody ever dared tell me off till this mad little girl in the apron, and I deserve it, I deserve it, I'm such a bad little millionaire!'

His mouth puckered and big tears rolled down his cheeks, mingling with the gravy stains.

'Never mind that,' said Marmalade. 'And we don't want any *soppy babies* here. Dry your eyes, get your elbows off the table, don't speak with your mouth full and eat up properly. I want to see *clean plates!*'

'Yes Nanny, sorry Nanny,' muttered Aristotle. He bowed

his head, took his elbows off the table, and started to clear his plate (even the cabbage, which he hated), trying very hard not to eat with his mouth open.

'And that goes for the rest of you lot too!' said Marmalade. And all the other millionaires did the same. Some of them had had strict English nannies and some of them hadn't, but when Aristotle Carioutabotl gets his elbows off the table, *everybody* gets his elbows off the table, and when Aristotle Carioutabotl cleans his plate, *everybody* cleans his plate.

No sound could be heard in the Ritz dining-room but the quiet clinking of the knives and forks and the clomping of Rufus's hooves as he and Marmalade walked between the tables inspecting.

'Right, cock,' said Marmalade. 'When you've eaten every scrap, you can pass the plates up quietly, take them into the kitchen and wash them up. The Head Chef will issue you with mops and aprons. And then, if you're *very* good, you *might* get some pudding!'

She paused, wondering whether she had gone too far. The millionaires stared at her in disbelief. They had never washed up in their lives, most of them.

'I say,' said a fat and pink-faced millionaire sitting just in front of Rufus. 'That's not on – I mean – well we're the customers – I mean dash it, customers don't wash up!'

'They do tonight, cock,' said Marmalade, and Rufus gave the pink-faced millionaire a moderate nudge on the back of his head that sent his face flying into his dinner.

'That's the way!' yelled Aristotle. 'Go it, Nanny! Go it, donkey!'

'Quiet!' said Marmalade. 'Little millionaires should be seen but not heard. Now, pass your plates up and into the kitchen with you!'

All the millionaires passed their plates up and trooped into the kitchen to wash up. They weren't very good at washing up, but there were a lot of them and after a while they started to enjoy themselves, making glob-glob noises with the champagne glasses, and putting foam on their faces and pretending to be Father Christmases. The waiters and the kitchen staff quite enjoyed it as well. They came out of the kitchen and lounged about at the tables, eating strawberries and drinking champagne.

After half an hour, Aristotle Carioutabotl came out of the kitchen. 'Please, Nanny,' he said. 'We've washed up all the plates. Is there anything else we can do?'

'Yes, cock,' said Marmalade. 'There's a lot of tramps in cardboard boxes out there in the cold. They haven't had a good nosh up for years. You can bring 'em in, and sit 'em down and buy 'em a big dinner, and you and your mates can serve it up!'

'Oh, Nanny! What a splendid idea!' said Aristotle Carioutabotl.

The manager threw the doors open and all the tramps shuffled in and sat down at the tables. Marmalade and Rufus

sat down with them, and the millionaires scurried about serving up a gigantic banquet. Marmalade had seventeen plates of strawberries and cream at five pounds a go, and Rufus had seven nosebags full of fresh asparagus at five pounds a stick, and the tramps all got stuck in and ate their heads off. After about three hours Marmalade put down her spoon.

'Right, cock,' she said. 'We're full.'

'Thank you, thank you,' said Aristotle Carioutabotl. 'This has been the most wonderful evening of my life!'

'You must be barmier than you look, cock,' said Marmalade Atkins. 'Manager! Bring him the bill!'

Aristotle Carioutabotl sat down at the table and the manager brought him the bill. The bill was about six yards long, it had so many items on it, and when Aristotle Carioutabotl got down to the bottom line (which is the bit you actually have to pay) he went white as a sheet. He tried turning the bill upside-down, but it looked just as bad that way.

'Is anything the matter, sir?' asked the manager.

'No, no,' said Aristotle Carioutabotl, in a rather panicky way. He sat there for a moment white and shaking, then an idea flashed into his mind. He looked around. Most of the tramps were asleep. The manager was busy with his calculator. The waiters were busy with the champagne. Rufus and Marmalade were leaning against each other, full as guns, and Rufus was snoring gently into his nosebag.

Aristotle Carioutabotl leapt to his feet. 'Mad Dog,' he shrieked, and raced for the front door yowling at the top of his voice. He was a fast little mover for a shipping millionaire, and he would have got away with it if Rufus had not suddenly woken up, heard the sound of what he took to be a heehaw zigzag, and launched into a heehaw zigzag of his own. Round the tables he went, heehawing at the top of his voice and kicking his back legs out, and he met Aristotle Carioutabotl in the doorway.

Aristotle Carioutabotl suddenly found he had to sit down on the floor, and did so. Rufus sat down too, staring at him in a mild and puzzled way.

'It's a fair cop,' said the millionaire. 'I'll pay. Suppose I'll have to sell one of my oil tankers.'

Then the Manager and the waiters came rushing up.

'Thank you, thank you,' said the Manager to Marmalade and Rufus. 'The Ritz Hotel is profoundly grateful to you both. We should like to offer you a little reward of some kind.'

'How about putting us up for a week or so?' said Marmalade.

'Certainly, certainly!' said the Manager.

'Free of charge?' said Marmalade.

'Of course, of course,' said the Manager, rather less enthusiastically.

'Thanks a lot, cock,' said Marmalade. 'The Golden Fleece Suite would suit us very nicely.'

Deborah Delora

Deborah Delora, she liked a bit of fun –
She went to the baker's and she bought a penny bun,
Dipped the bun in treacle and threw it at her teacher,
Deborah Delora! What a wicked creature!

Anon.

Friends and Brothers

Dick King-Smith

'You say that word just once more,' said William to Charlie, 'and I'll hit you.'

Charlie said it.

William hit him.

Charlie then let out a screech and kicked William on the shin, and William bellowed.

William and Charlie's mother came rushing in like a whirlwind, with a face like thunder.

'You two will drive me mad!' she stormed. 'All you do is fight, all day long!'

'William hit me,' said Charlie.

'Why did you hit him, William?'

'Because Charlie keeps on saying the same word. Whatever I say, he says the same word, over and over again. Anyway, he kicked me.'

'Will hit me first,' said Charlie.

'William,' said his mother, 'you are not to hit Charlie. He is younger than you and much smaller. The next time you do, I shall hit you.'

'You didn't ought to, Mum,' said William.

'Why not?'

'I'm younger than you and much smaller.'

'Absolutely,' said Charlie.

'There you are!' shouted William madly. 'That's the word! Whatever I say, he just says "Absolutely". He doesn't even know what it means.'

'Absolutely,' said Charlie.

William let out a yell of rage and rushed at his brother with his fists clenched. Charlie dodged behind his mother, who held the furious William at arm's length.

'Now *stop* it, the pair of you!' she said. 'William, you stop attacking Charlie, and Charlie, you stop annoying Will. I cannot stand one more minute of being shut in this house with you two. Get your bikes. We'll go to the Park.'

William stumped off, limping slightly from the kick, and shouting angrily, 'It's not fair!'

From behind his mother's back, Charlie's face appeared. Silently he mouthed the word 'Absolutely'.

In the Park, William rode his BMX at top speed. He felt the need to be all by himself, miles from anybody. The roads in the Park were full of steep switchback slopes, and William swooped down them flat out. Like a lot of elder brothers, he felt he had had a raw deal.

Charlie, meanwhile, was trying to see how slowly he could pedal without falling off. He had not long inherited William's old bike and was fascinated by the problems of balance. This was much more fun than a tricycle. Like a lot of younger brothers, he had forgotten all about the recent row, and was singing happily to himself. Then he came to the top of one of the steepest slopes. He grinned, and bent low over the handlebars.

His mother, walking some way behind, saw the small figure disappear from view. A moment later, a dreadful wailing started her running hard.

Halfway down the slope, Charlie lay sprawled in the road, the old bike beside him, one wheel still spinning. His face, she saw when she reached him, was covered in blood. There was a deep cut across his forehead and a set of long scratches, gravel-studded, down one cheek.

At that moment William came flying back down the reverse slope and skidded to a halt, wide-eyed with horror at the scene.

'What happened?' he said miserably.

'I don't know. He must have touched the brakes and gone straight over the handlebars. Listen carefully, Will. We must

get him to hospital quickly – that cut's going to need stitches. I'm going to carry him to the nearest Park gate, that one over there, and try and stop a car to give us a lift. Can you wheel both bikes and stick them out of sight in those bushes, and then run and catch me up?'

'Yes, Mum,' said William.

He looked at his brother's face. Charlie was still crying, but quietly now.

'He'll be all right won't he?' William said.

Twenty-four hours later Charlie, recovered now from the shock of his accident, was jabbering away nineteen to the dozen.

He remembered little of the actual crash, or of his treatment in hospital, the stitching of the cut and the cleaning-up of his gravelly face. It was very swollen now, so that one side of him didn't look like Charlie at all, but his voice was as loud and piercing as ever as he plied his brother with endless questions.

'Did you see me come off, Will?'

'No.'

'I went right over the handlebars, didn't I?'

'Suppose so.'

'How fast d'you think I was going, Will?'

'I don't know.'

'A hundred miles an hour, d'you think?' squeaked Charlie excitedly.

'I expect so, Charles,' said William in a kindly voice. 'You looked an awful mess when I got there.'

'Lots of blood, Will?'

'Yes. Ugh, it was horrible.'

'Then what happened?'

'Well, Mum ran all the way to the nearest gate carrying you, and a kind lady in a car stopped and gave us all a lift to the hospital.'

'And then they stitched me up!' said Charlie proudly.

'Yes.'

'Did you see them stitching me up, Will?'

'No, Charles.'

'I expect it was a huge great needle,' said Charlie happily. 'You've never had six stitches, have you, Will?'

'No,' said William. 'You were jolly brave, Charlie,' he said. 'You can have a go on my BMX when you're better.'

'I can't reach the pedals,' Charlie said.

'Oh. Well, you can take a picture with my Instamatic if you like.'

'Can I really, Will?'

'And you can borrow my Swiss Army knife for a bit.'

'Can I really?'

'Yes,' said William. He put his hand in his pocket and pulled out a rather squidgy-looking bar of chocolate.

'And you can have half of this,' he said.

'Gosh, thanks, Will!'

William and Charlie's mother put her head round the door, wondering at the unaccustomed silence, and saw her sons sitting side by side on Charlie's bed, chewing chocolate. William actually had his arm round Charlie's shoulders.

'Look what I've got, Mum,' said Charlie with his mouth full.

'Did you give him some of yours, Will?' said his mother.

'Naturally,' said William loftily. 'We're friends and brothers.'

Another day went by, and Charlie was definitely better. His face was much less swollen, his spirits high, his voice shriller yet.

He had made up a song about his exploits, which he sang, endlessly and very loudly.

> *'Who came rushing down the hill?*
> *Charlie boy!*
> *Who had such an awful spill?*
> *Charlie boy!*
> *Who came down with a terrible thud,*
> *Covered in mud and covered in blood?*
> *Charlie, Charlie, Charlie boy!'*

William, as he occasionally did, had an attack of earache, painful enough without Charlie's singing.

'Charles,' he said as the friend and brother was just about to come rushing down the hill for the twentieth time, 'd'you think you could keep a bit quiet?'

'Why?' shouted Charlie at the top of his voice.

'Because I've got earache.'

'Oh,' said Charlie in a whisper. 'Oh, sorry, Will. Does it hurt a lot?'

'Yes,' said William, white-faced, 'it does.'

For the rest of the day Charlie tiptoed about the house, occasionally asking William if he needed anything, and, if he did, fetching it. He guarded his brother's peace and quiet fiercely, frowning angrily at his mother when she dropped a saucepan on the kitchen floor.

'Hullo, Charlie boy!' shouted his father on his return from work. 'How's the poor old face?'

'Don't make such a noise, Dad!' hissed Charlie furiously. 'Will's got earache.'

It was now a week since Charlie's accident, a week of harmony and brotherly love.

Charlie's face was now miles better and William's earache quite gone.

They were drawing pictures, at the kitchen table, with felt pens.

'Charles,' said William. 'Can I borrow your red? Mine's run out.'

'No,' said Charlie.

'Why not? You're not using it.'

'Yes I am,' said Charlie, picking up his red felt and colouring with it.

'You did that to be annoying,' said William angrily.

The word 'annoying' rang a bell with Charlie, and he grinned and nodded and said, 'Absolutely!'

'Charlie!' said William between his teeth. 'Don't start that again or I'll hit you!'

'You can't,' said Charlie. 'I've got a bad face.'

'I'll hit you all the same,' said William.

'I'll shout in your bad ear,' said Charlie, 'and d'you know what I'll shout?'

'What?'

'ABSOLUTELY!!' yelled Charlie and scuttled out of the room with William in hot pursuit, as life returned to normal.

Acknowledgements

The editors and publishers gratefully acknowledge the following for permission to reproduce copyright stories in this book:

Blackie and Son Ltd for 'Marmalade and Rufus at the Ritz' by Andrew Davies, reprinted from *Marmalade Atkins Hits the Big Time*, copyright © Andrew Davies, 1984; Unwin Hyman and Penguin Books Ltd for 'Veruca in the Nut Room' by Roald Dahl, reprinted from *Charlie and the Chocolate Factory*, copyright © Roald Dahl, 1964; Faber and Faber Ltd for 'The Secret' by Gene Kemp, reprinted from *The Well*, copyright © Gene Kemp, 1984; Heinemann Ltd for 'Friends and Brothers' by Dick King-Smith, reprinted from *Friends and Brothers*, copyright © Dick King-Smith, 1987; Hodder and Stoughton for 'When Emil Got His Head Stuck in the Soup Tureen' by Astrid Lindgren, reprinted from *Emil in the Soup Tureen*, copyright © Astrid Lindgren, 1963; first English translation copyright © 1970 Brockhampton Press Ltd (now part of Hodder and Stoughton); Heinemann Ltd for 'Temper, Temper . . .' by Jules Older, reprinted from *Hankprank and Hot Henrietta*, copyright © Jules Older, 1984; Viking Kestrel for 'The Conker as Hard as a Diamond' by Chris Powling, reprinted from *The Conker as Hard as a Diamond*, copyright © Chris Powling, 1984; Blackie and Son Ltd for 'The Croco-bus' by Martin Waddell, reprinted from *Harriet and the Crocodiles*, copyright © Martin Waddell, 1986; Bodley Head for 'Castles in the Sand' by David Henry Wilson, reprinted from *Beside the Sea with Jeremy James*, copyright © David Henry Wilson, 1980.